GW00838391

The Earned Value
Management Compass

A product of the Association for Project Management
Earned Value Management Specific Interest Group (SIG)

Association for Project Management
Ibis House, Regent Park
Summerleys Road, Princes Risborough
Buckinghamshire
HP27 9LE

British Library Cataloguing in Publication Data is available

ISBN 10: 1-903494-33-8
ISBN 13: 978-1-903494-33-2

Cover design by Fountainhead Creative Consultants

Typeset by RefineCatch Limited, Bungay, Suffolk

Contents

Foreword

More and more companies are saying that they use earned value (EV) as part of their project control.

However, use of earned value can run from full organisational US ANSI 748 accreditation to recognising that there is an earned value button available in your personal copy of Microsoft® Project.

This is potentially confusing and there is a very high risk of misunderstanding and disappointed expectations between stakeholders.

The APM Earned Value Specific Interest Group (SIG) recognises that EV principles and the benefits they can bring to project control may be applied in a variety of ways. In some cases the principles are being applied without knowing that they are part of earned value. The key is to understand how and where earned value principles are being applied and to encourage them.

The earned value management (EVM) compass has been developed so that a clear picture can be obtained of how earned value is being used currently. An assessment can then be made of how well that meets the actual requirement for earned value; whether that is to meet a standard, a customer or an internal organisational requirement. A route map to close the gap between *as is* and *to be* can then be plotted planned and managed.

Now, when it is stated that earned value is in use, the compass can provide a way for all involved to have a common understanding of what that really means.

The compass can be used in a variety of project control situations (not just earned value). Here are some suggestions:

- Maturity model.
- Audit tool.
- Assurance tool.
- Management tool.
- As part of an external team's review or as a personal self-assessment exercise.

It is flexible. Please use it and let the SIG know how you get on.

Steve Wake
Chairman, APM Earned Value Specific Interest Group

iv

Acknowledgements

The EVM compass was developed by a subgroup of the APM Earned Value Specific Interest Group (SIG), with contributions from Steve Wake (SIG chairman), Mike Burke, Ewan Glen, John Flaherty, Paul Kidston, Simon Springate, Alan Bye, John Cox, Mick Higgins and Alex Davis.

Review and testing of the compass has been completed by the wider APM Earned Value SIG membership and cross-industry volunteers and we are extremely grateful to all the individuals who took part in this.

The EVM Compass

INTRODUCTION

How do you measure an organisation's capability in implementing and applying earned value management (EVM) across its projects? For example, what is the subset of the *Earned Value Management: APM Guidelines* (or ANSI/EIA 748 requirements) that are sufficient to initiate an EVM system? How do you know your potential alliance partner or subcontractor has a competent EVM system? How do you know whether its constituent elements such as scheduling, cost collection and adequate supplier project control are in place?

  The EVM compass maturity model provides a step-by-step means to understanding the *as is* EVM condition and referencing it against a *to be* condition. The model uses a common framework and can be used for the assessment of a single project or to benchmark and compare the relative strengths of various projects across an organisation. It gives EVM system reviewers a consistent method of assessing projects.

  This document is intended to be used in conjunction with the *Earned Value Management: APM Guidelines*.

FUNDAMENTAL CONCEPTS

The EVM compass is intended to provide a defined means of establishing and improving project control capability. The EVM compass is intended to support projects or organisations by improving their project control and EVM processes.

  The project control processes should be well understood throughout a mature project or organisation, usually through documentation and training. The processes should be continually monitored and improved. As a project or organisation gains in EVM process maturity, it formalises its processes via policies, standards, and organisational structures. It also builds an infrastructure and a corporate culture that support the methods, practices and procedures of the project/organisation so they continue to function long after those who originally defined them have moved on.

  Working within this environment, the fundamental concepts of the EVM compass are that it:

- provides a comprehensive and systematic review of **project** EVM maturity;
- uses a **common framework** that supports either the assessment of a single project or allows organisations to benchmark and compare the relative strengths of their various projects, identifying systemic problems and allowing sharing of best practice;

- provides a defined means to support projects in **establishing and improving project control capability**;
- allows projects to **reference the** *as is* EVM condition **with the** *to be* condition;
- gives EVM system reviewers a **consistent** method of assessing projects that can be repeated over a period of time, recognising that target performance levels may change;
- allows organisations to **establish their own target performance level** (rather than define it for them);
- is open to a degree of **customisation** such that its application can be tailored to the needs of an individual organisation, whether this is through revisions to the criteria or the application of weightings to the criteria.

HOW IS THE COMPASS USED FOR ASSESSMENT?

In the context of this framework, the EVM compass is a comprehensive and systematic review of a project's EVM maturity. This can be used to aid process improvement by identifying shortfalls against the target standard.

The review is conducted using a maturity grid that outlines performance levels against 25 attributes of an EVM system. A target standard should be established for the project or projects within an organisation at the outset and the maturity at the time of review related to this target standard. The target standard to be achieved will typically be agreed with a customer of the project or within an organisation. It is for individual projects/organisations to set their target standards. However, customers who require full ANSI 748 compliance are unlikely to be satisfied with maturity below level 3.

When using the EVM compass, it is often beneficial to take a realistic and pragmatic approach. Where an organisation doesn't implement full EVM, as outlined in ANSI 748, then the maturity level achieved will be less than if they did, with it being likely that several of the products identified will not be available. This may be appropriate for that organisation.

The assessment process allows the project to clearly discern its strengths and weaknesses, and should culminate in planned improvement actions which are then monitored for progress.

The frequency of reviews is a decision for the project or organisation.

WHAT ARE THE BENEFITS?

Using the EVM compass maturity framework for assessment should deliver a range of benefits, including:

- identifying your organisation's strengths and weaknesses;
- providing a highly structured, fact-based approach to identifying and assessing your project and measuring progress periodically;

- creating a common language and conceptual framework for the way you manage and improve EVM on your project and, if applicable, projects within your organisation;
- educating people in your project on the fundamental elements of EVM and how they relate to their roles and responsibilities;
- involving people at all levels in process improvement;
- ranking EVM project maturity within an organisation or across the supply chain;
- identifying and allowing the sharing of best practice across projects within an organisation;
- using it to assess and present the findings from a variety of EVM reviews in a format that is easy to understand;
- facilitating comparisons with other projects;
- supporting the development of your business plan and strategy.

ASSESSMENT – THE GENERAL PROCESS

There is no single right way to perform the assessment using the maturity grid; the primary factors that determine the right approach for your organisation are its current culture and the desired outcomes from the assessment exercise. Different approaches deliver different benefits. Whichever approach is used, the key point to remember is that assessment is about the continuous improvement of your project.

Greatest value may be achieved from an assessment if it involves someone who has a working knowledge of the implementation and operation of an EVM system. This ensures that the assessment can be completed with an understanding of the nuances between the different maturity levels for each of the attributes that are scored.

The assessment can be performed in a number of different ways:

- Self assessment – from within the project.
- Peer assessment – by other teams within the organisation.
- Independent assessment – by reviewers external to the project.

The steps involved in the assessment are outlined in the figure below.

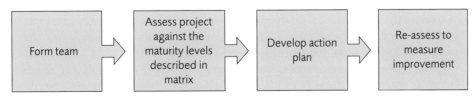

Figure 1: **Four-step assessment method**

While the assessment is valuable, the most critical phase of the process is action planning and implementation. Having completed the diagnostic phase, you may wish to consider your response to the following questions:

- What identified strengths must we maintain to maximum effect?
- What identified strengths do we develop and exploit even further?
- What identified areas for improvement do we acknowledge, but not pursue because they are not key to our business?
- What identified areas for improvement do we acknowledge and are vital for us to address?
- How are we going to monitor progress against the agreed improvement actions?

The actions that are identified should be captured in a plan, with clearly defined responsibilities and timescales for their implementation. To help with the prioritisation of the actions a grid such as that shown overleaf may be of benefit.

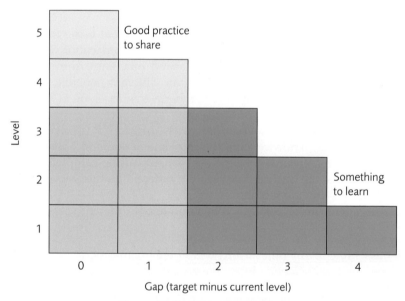

Figure 2: **Action prioritisation**

The grid may be used by taking your current score and identifying where you sit on the vertical axis. By then taking your current score away from your target score you may identify your position on the horizontal axis. As the shade of blue darkens, the priority of actions increases.

Where a project scores predominately light blue there is potential to share learning with other projects in the organisation that may not be performing so well.

ASSESSMENT – PRESENTING THE RESULTS

The presentation of results from the assessment may be tailored to meet the needs of specific organisations. As a general rule, presentation of the full set of results for the 25 criteria lends itself to use by project control staff. Summarised results, such as at the level of maturity stages, tend to be more appropriate for presentation to management staff.

Full set of results

Figure 3 provides examples of two presentation formats, (a) radar plot and (b) bar chart, for the full set of results. While detailed, they allow easy comparison of current performance against the target performance level. By including the results of assessments from multiple projects it becomes possible with the bar chart to identify systemic problems that can be addressed if desired.

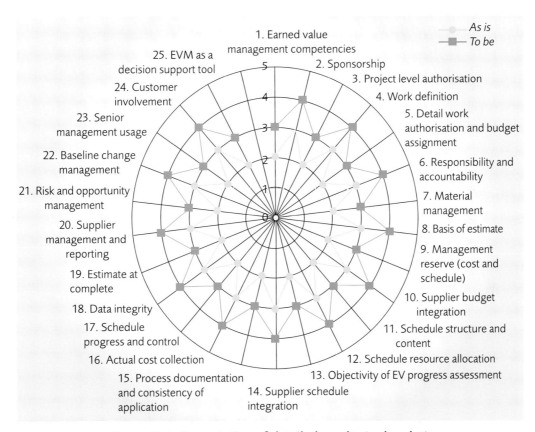

Figure 3(a): **Presentation of detailed results (radar plot)**

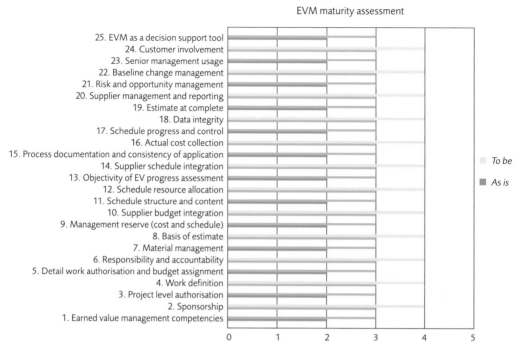

Figure 3(b): **Bar chart**

Summarised results

Figure 4 provides an example of a summarised results plot. Presenting the results of assessments conducted across numerous projects becomes simpler at this level and differences between current and target performance levels may be highlighted.

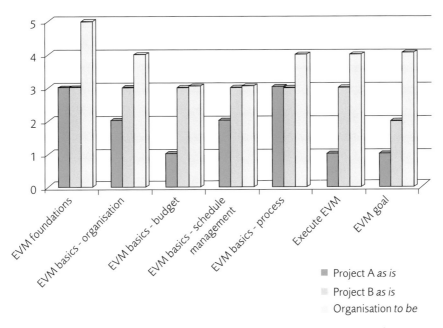

Figure 4: **Presentation of summarised results (bar chart only)**

IMPLEMENTATION ROADMAP – EVM PROCESS MATURITY STAGES

The structure of the EVM compass aims to reflect the stages that a project will pass through when implementing an EVM system (Figure 5). An organisation that has little experience of establishing an EVM system should focus on the stages in the order outlined below to achieve the greatest benefit. Where an organisation has more experience of using EVM it is likely that the initial stages will be established and focus may be on the latter ones. The stages are:

1. **EVM foundations**. The first step in establishing an effective EVM system is to establish the correct foundations. Without appropriate sponsorship and the development of the correct competencies EVM systems are more likely to fail.
2. **EVM basics**. The attributes within the EVM basics stage form the building blocks of an effective EVM system. This maturity stage is concerned with ensuring that these meet the needs of the project, formally controlling the scope of work and associated delivery schedule and budget within a system that has defined processes.
3. **Execute EVM**. Having established the foundations and performance baseline it is possible to start to manage using EVM. This maturity stage is

concerned with assessing the effectiveness of the processes followed though the delivery stage of a project.

4. **EVM goal**. The ultimate aim of an EVM system is to establish the information generated by the system as a decision support tool.

Building up from the foundations it provides a logical path for EVM implementation. The compass measures the maturity of the implementation attributes as a project establishes the basics, before starting to execute EVM and finally using EVM as a decision support tool (the goal).

The attributes within each of the stages are outlined in detail in the guidance text that follows.

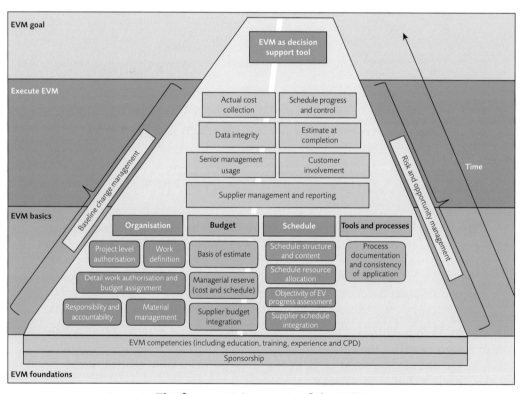

Figure 5: **The four maturity stages of the EVM compass**

Guidance information

INTRODUCTION

This section aims to provide guidance to support the use of the EVM compass maturity assessment tables. For each of the four stages the following explanatory text is provided for the underpinning attributes. This text outlines:

- *The aim* – the objective of the attribute;
- *The reason* – why the attribute is important;
- *Guidance information* – additional information to assist users who are less familiar with the implementation and utilisation of earned value management systems.

EVM FOUNDATIONS

Attribute 1 – earned value management competencies

Aim:

- To ensure that the project team has the appropriate competencies to implement and manage using an earned value management system.

Reason:

- EVM is often a new process to a project or business and requires appropriate training and education for its implementation to be a success. Implementation and operation of an EVM system can be a complex exercise and can be facilitated by the use of experienced resources.

Guidance information:

It is important that training and support are provided during EVM implementation and that on-going training is also available. The team members should be trained in EVM techniques appropriate to their role within the project team.

  Implementation of EVM is best facilitated by using resources with previous implementation experience. Learned experience from other projects is also a valuable source of information.

Attribute 2 – sponsorship

Aim:

- To ensure that there is clear and visible EVM sponsorship for the project from within the delivery organisation.

Reason:

- It is important that the implementation and execution of EVM is sponsored at an appropriate level within the project/organisation.

Guidance information:

The introduction of EVM may cause the need for a significant cultural change, which must be led with senior management support and sponsorship. This should be communicated throughout the entire project structure. The understanding and commitment of the entire project team and organisational functional areas is vital for success, and hence there is a need for comprehensive communication outlining the nature of EVM, the aim and objectives of the implementation.

EVM BASICS

Attribute 3 – project level authorisation

Aim:

- To ensure that the project has been given appropriate approval and authority to proceed.

Reason:

- The project should be formally approved by the responsible organisation. This approval should indicate the overall budget available and assign delivery responsibility/authority onto the key individuals within the project team. It should also indicate the sponsor within the organisation.

Guidance information:

Prior to commencement of work on the project, the approval authority should formally sanction the project to proceed and assign the required level of responsibility, authority and accountability (RAA) to the project manager. To further delegate this RAA to the team delivering the project, a responsibility assignment matrix (RAM) is used.

   The RAM process is principally concerned with defining the work to be done, as a work breakdown structure (WBS), and assigning that work to specific parts of the project's organisation via the organisational breakdown structure (OBS). The WBS and OBS should be aligned and combined to produce a concise RAM, an example of which is shown below.

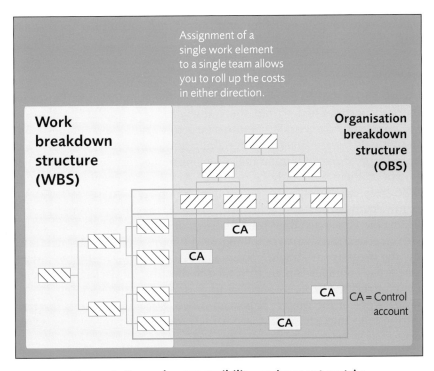

Figure 6: **Example responsibility assignment matrix**

Within the RAM, each element of work is assigned to an organisational element and a single person within the organisation. This is regarded as an individual control account (CA). Each control account will be owned by a control account manager (CAM) and will contain lower level, detailed work packages (or near term work) and also summarised planning packages (or far term work).

Attribute 4 – work definition

Aim:

- To ensure that the full scope of work associated with the project has been broken into manageable elements in a manner that supports performance reporting.

Reason:

- The project scope of work should be broken into manageable elements in a manner that supports delivery of work and performance reporting. Failure to break down work appropriately can lead to difficulties with assigning a single point of accountability for delivery of the work and also lead to confusing, conflicting and sometimes incomplete performance data.

Guidance information:

All work authorised to be performed under the contract must be formally authorised and defined within the framework of a logical breakdown of work, normally via a work breakdown structure (WBS) and will be assigned to individuals responsible for undertaking that work.

The WBS provides a common management framework for all project activities, and so there must only be one WBS for any single contract. The WBS will be cross-referenced with the contract statement of work or a statement of requirements to ensure the full scope of work has been covered.

The level to which a WBS is broken down depends upon the complexity of the contract and the level of detail required for effective management. Essentially, the breakdown should continue until all contract requirements and business requirements can be attributed to meaningful packages of work.

In any project the WBS is of critical importance because it defines not only how the work of the project is broken down, but also provides the framework for collecting actual cost, reporting progress and measuring achievement.

Attribute 5 – detail work authorisation and budget assignment

Aim:

- To ensure that all distributed work has an associated budget, has been assigned to an individual with delivery responsibility, and that all work is authorised before it commences.

Reason:

- Every package of work within the WBS should be assigned an agreed budget for its completion that is commensurate with the scope of work to be delivered (i.e. is sufficient to cover labour, material and other direct costs that will be incurred while delivering the work). Before work commences, the associated budget and schedule must be authorised to indicate approval to proceed (typically this would open associated cost booking numbers).

Guidance information:

The detail work authorisation and budget assignment process ensures that every package of work within the WBS is assigned an agreed budget for its completion. This is part of the formal authorisation process that allows work to commence against the agreed schedule baseline for each control account - and therefore the project as a whole. These budgets may consist of a labour element (resources) and/or materials element and will be assigned to all work packages (WP) and planning packages (PP). However, it is recommended that the different cost types should be kept in separate WPs/PPs where possible.

To manage the completion of work against work packages they will usually only be opened when they have been formally authorised (typically when they are due to commence in the next few months) and will be closed when they are completed. This also helps to ensure that full control is maintained over the work package and no work is completed against it, either before it is authorised or after it has been deemed to be complete and full earned value claimed.

Attribute 6 – responsibility and accountability

Aim:

- To ensure that identified staff within the project team have appropriately delegated and documented responsibilities and accountabilities and that these have been communicated.

Reason:

- It is important that staff within the project are clear on what they are responsible for delivering, and that they have the necessary authority. Whilst achieving this it is also crucial that accountability rests with single individuals.

Guidance information:

The project team (inclusive of control account managers) have responsibility for the delivery of the project. It is essential that individuals within the project have a clear definition and understanding of their terms of reference and that these are clearly understood by those within the project and the associated functional organisational areas. A control account manager (CAM) has management responsibility for ensuring that the defined scope of work for a control account is achieved to the budget, timescale and quality standards in accordance with the project requirements. They manage the control account as a contract between themselves and the project manager / project director.

Typical CAM terms of reference are for someone:

- who is *accountable* for ensuring that the defined scope of work for a discrete control account is achieved to budget and timescales;
- with the delegated *authority* to manage the deployment and mix of resources required to achieve budget and timescales;
- who is *empowered* to manage the internal contract between the project and the organisation performing the work;
- who is *experienced* in project delivery/management and can strike the balance between technical and business requirements;
- who can demonstrate adequate knowledge, *commitment* and ownership of their control accounts.

Attribute 7 – material management

Aim:

- To ensure that the material budget is included in the earned value management system (EVMS) to support accurate performance reporting.

Reason:

- To establish the complete project budget and enable material performance management, it is essential to ensure that the material elements are contained within the performance measurement baseline.

Guidance information:

The management of purchased material/services covers the processes and activities that directly affect the purchase of bill of material items or services from external suppliers. These elements should all be captured in the EVMS with appropriate progress measurement and actual cost collection techniques.

Attribute 8 – basis of estimate

Aim:

- To ensure that the rationale for producing the estimates that underpin the budget and schedule data are contained in a formal document.

Reason:

- The basis of estimate (BoE), accompanied with related assumptions, ensures that the project can demonstrate how it developed its budget and schedule. It aids future reviews of the budget, which is particularly important if the staff involved in their original development are no longer available.

In reviewing this area it is important to understand the CAM's role in formulating the proposal estimate/budget for the effort. A number of questions should be asked:

a) How did they arrive at the proposed estimates?
b) Are there backup worksheets to give more detail?
c) Was there a negotiation process for the budgets after the contract was awarded?
d) Is the budget adequate and what risks are there in achieving the work within budget?

The data justifying the responses to these questions should be formally documented in the BoE file.

Attribute 9 – management reserve (cost and schedule)

Aim:

- To ensure that management reserve is identified, documented and approved, and is subject to formal change approval when drawn upon by the project.

Reason:

- Projects should have a separately identified management reserve budget that can be used for unplanned scope. The management reserve budget will typically be sized based upon the risk exposure of the project as represented in the risk register.

Guidance information:

Management reserve (MR) is set aside for project management control purposes only. It is not a contingency that can be eliminated by the customer during subsequent negotiations, nor can it be used by the customer to absorb the cost of contract changes.

  MR is derived during the budgeting process. It is held separately for future allocation to control accounts (using the project change process) and will be used, if required, to cover increased work-scope requirements for unforeseen changes that fall within the overall scope of the contract. For more detail on the interfacing of risk and EVM, reference should be made to the *Interfacing Risk and Earned Value Management* guide on this subject.

Attribute 10 – supplier budget integration

Aim:

- To ensure that the suppliers budget is included in the EVMS to support accurate performance reporting.

Reason:

- To establish the complete project budget and enable supplier performance management it is essential to ensure that the supplier budget elements are contained within the performance measurement baseline.

Guidance information:

The nature of budget integration will depend on the earned value approach prescribed for the supplier. This could be full EVM requirements flowed down to the supplier to report budgeted cost for work performed (BCWP) and actual cost of work performed (ACWP) periodically, milestone based EV measurement where a milestone payment plan linked to physical progress is agreed with the supplier and this forms the BCWS, or, for commodities and consumables, a BCWS is established based on the planned receipt.

The approach defined will depend upon the nature of the item being pro-cured, the criticality and the risk/opportunities. Where full EVM is flowed down to the supplier, the contract should clearly define the requirement.

For more guidance on the selection of the best approach reference should be made to *Earned Value Management: APM Guidelines.*

Attribute 11 – schedule structure and content

Aim:

- To ensure that there is a robust, time-phased, logically-linked set of activities and milestones that show how products/outputs will be delivered.

Reason:

- The critical objectives for any project are the delivery of the product to time, specification and cost. As such, a schedule or suite of schedules needs to be created to display the logic, durations and interdependencies of all project activities.

Guidance information:

The schedule should cover all work-scope and will include all master mile-stones (i.e. payment milestones, contract deliverables and key programme milestones). There will be a clear link between the established control accounts and work packages created within the EVM system and the activities within the schedule.

The schedule should enable the critical path to be clearly visible. Supplier schedules should be integrated at a level of detail dependent on the type of scope or service being purchased. The amount of detail within the schedule will be dependent on the nature and scale of the project.

Attribute 12 – schedule resource allocation

Aim:

- To ensure that the schedule is resourced, and that resource planning is undertaken.

Reason:

- The schedule should be resourced with the amount and type of resource required to deliver the project, typically using a resource breakdown structure to identify the skill types within an organisation. Resource levelling should be conducted to ensure that the resources required to deliver the project are available when required.

Guidance information:

The schedule resource requirements should be understood within the context of the wider resource requirements of the organisation. Use of the schedule should allow proactive, flexible resource management to optimise the utilisation of the workforce within an organisation.

Attribute 13 – objectivity of EV progress assessment

Aim:

- To ensure that appropriate earned value techniques (EVT) are applied.

Reason:

- To accurately assess progress it is important to assign the most appropriate EVT to activities/work packages. Without this, the performance reported may fail to reflect actual performance achieved.

Guidance information:

The EVT is the technique used to measure achievement; also known as the budgeted cost of work performed (BWCP) or earned value (EV). The optimum EVT must be assigned to individual work packages. The vast majority of work packages on a project should be a discrete type as these provide the most objective measure of the value of *in progress* work.

The EVT chosen must best represent the effort to be accomplished and provide the most appropriate method for planning, scheduling and evaluating performance. Work Packages should be identified as one of 3 types:

1) **Discrete** tasks – that have a specific end product or result.
2) **Apportioned** – factored effort that can be directly related to other identified discrete tasks.
3) **Level of effort (LOE)** – support/management type of work which does not result in a final product – performance/achievement cannot be measured since there is no tangible output.

The earned value techniques for each work package on a project should be documented, and the WBS should be structured such that the amount of LOE on a project is capable of being reported.

For more guidance on the selection of EVTs, reference should be made to *Earned Value Management: APM Guidelines*.

Attribute 14 – supplier schedule integration

Aim:

• To ensure that project schedules reflect supplier activities and deliverables, giving visibility of the interaction between the schedules of all parties.

Reason:

• To enable supplier progress tracking and fully understand the interdependencies, it is essential to ensure that the supplier schedules are contained within the project master schedule.

Guidance information:

The way in which subcontractor effort is integrated into the baseline will differ according to its importance to the project. The distinction between major and minor subcontractor should be based upon factors such as equipment value, criticality, or risk to the project (e.g. single source supply) and/or whether they are an 'off the shelf' supplier or not.

It is essential to ensure that sub-contractors' schedules are represented within the project master schedule to an appropriate level of detail, and that there is a process for reporting and managing the sub-contracted effort. The requirements for sub-contractor schedule provision and reporting should be defined in their contract.

In the event of progress payments being used, a definition of the method of validating the supplier's performance should be recorded in the purchase order (or contract).

Schedules on a major project can be very large and complex; decisions have to be taken as to the level of detail to be incorporated into the project's master schedule. If there is too much detail, the maintenance of the plan becomes a burdensome overhead, whilst if there is insufficient detail, the exact status of the project is difficult to ascertain.

It is usually the key deliverables that need to be monitored and controlled by the contractor. The focus of supplier schedules is typically:

- payment milestones (ideally one per period);
- key events and/or way points (identified by period where possible);
- deliverables into the contractor;
- deliverables to other sub-contractors (interface milestones).

If milestone based EVM is being used, identified milestones will be allocated a budget/resource, based on the agreed payment to the sub-contractor – ideally following the agreed payment profile (refer to Attribute 10 – supplier budget integration). Budgeted milestones will be time-phased to create a BCWS for the subcontractor.

Attribute 15 – process documentation and consistency of application

Aim:

- To ensure that the EVM processes are formally described and documented to allow consistent application.

Reason:

- Documented processes can be communicated to all relevant stakeholders, ensuring consistent understanding and application.

Guidance information:

Formal process documentation should be created and be in operational use for all the EVM processes to an appropriate level of detail. It is important to document processes and procedures to enable continued operation of the process as new people join the project.

Where generic EVM processes are in use they may be tailored with guidelines to meet specific local requirements in the form of local project/process instructions for different projects. A pragmatic balance should be reached between any internal procedures and external contract-specified standards. Any local project instructions are under configuration control.

EXECUTE EVM

Attribute 16 – actual cost collection

Aim:

- To ensure that costs are collected at a level appropriate for performance reporting and that they can be reconciled with the accounting system.

Reason:

- It is important to ensure accuracy of cost collection and ensure that it is related to the correct activity within the activity/work package. Without this information the project will not fully understand how much it has cost to perform the authorised work.

Guidance information:

The accounting processes ensure that complete and accurate cost information is collected in a timely manner, to enable the transfer of actual cost information into the project control system's cost reporting tool (by period).

Costs will be associated with the planned work and will be recorded at activity, work package or control account level, and will be rolled-up to provide actual costs across the control account(s) and at the summary project level. The creation of booking or charge numbers, matched to the discrete aspects of the WBS, will also make it possible to measure progress/achievement in a meaningful manner (against the baseline plan). This will facilitate effective financial control of the project by enabling the organisation to identify the full cost associated with the project activity and, through linkage with the recording of progress against 'tasks', to identify the estimated costs at completion for the planned work remaining.

Direct costs are accumulated as labour man hours and non-labour pounds against the relevant booking or charge numbers. Across the project, the project control system's source collection systems will collect information and feed it into the cost ledger. The appropriate charging rates will be applied to labour hours to give a complete picture of the actual cost of the work performed. Indirect costs should also be captured at a level appropriate to allow their effective management.

Once the actual spend is available, all CAMs are responsible for verifying that they are both accurate and a true reflection of the actual costs of performing the work in that period.

Material costs should also be collected in the same period as the earned value is claimed. This may require the use of estimated actuals or accruals.

A process to check the accuracy of the actual costs should be developed and performed periodically. Corrections to actual costs should be appropriately documented.

If there are differences between the finance systems and the EVMS it should be possible to identify and determine the reason for the differences.

Attribute 17 – schedule progress and control

Aim:

- To ensure that the schedule is updated and analysed to capture progress and determine the performance against the baseline, enabling informed management actions.

• Establishing earned value performance requires the schedule progress to be captured on a periodic basis.

Every period, schedule progress and achievement (i.e. earned value) are collected and processed. Schedule variances against the baseline should be determined and reported. Critical path analysis of the current schedule and baseline schedule should be performed. Float should also be determined. As a result of the analysis information, management actions (corrective actions) are determined and implemented.

Schedule progress and control will also allow the impact to current resource plans to be evaluated and an estimate to complete to be generated for the remaining work.

Attribute 18 – data integrity

• To ensure that data is checked for accuracy.

• To provide confidence that it is accurate enough to support management decisions.

Checking processes should be in place to identify errors in the EVM data set. Any adjustments required must be to correct errors. Any financial transfers that are required should be made in the period following the error. Genuine cost variances should not be disguised through this process

Attribute 19 – estimate at complete (EAC)

• To ensure that the project generates a valid estimate at complete (including cost and schedule).

• The EAC provides an indication of the final funding requirements for the project, in addition to the likely completion date. (See also Attribute 17 – schedule progress and control)

Guidance information:

There are two main types of EAC:

- a CAM estimate* of the resources over time required to complete the work package
- independent estimates based upon standard EV calculations.

When establishing an ETC the following aspects should be considered:

- Past performance (efficiency) and trends.
- Costs incurred to date.
- Commitments placed (to date and potential future).
- Required efficiency to 'recover' variances.
- Technical assessment of remaining activities.
- Anticipated future efficiency (should relate to past performance).
- Forecast of schedule (time) to complete activity.
- Associated risks with remaining activity.
- Future economic conditions, e.g. rate changes, escalation indices, revised supplier contracts.
- Previous ETC trend.

Independent estimate: there is a range of standard independent estimates at complete (IEAC) calculation formulae that can be used to identify the potential project out-turn based upon performance to date. These are outlined in the *Earned Value Management: APM Guidelines.*

The CAM EAC should be compared to the standard IEAC calculations that are based on previous performance to provide a check on their realism.

Attribute 20 – supplier management and reporting

Aim:

- To ensure that supplier performance reporting is aligned with the requirements of the project, to enable effective supplier management.

Reason:

- Significant areas of projects are often managed and delivered by suppliers. It is important that these suppliers report relevant, agreed progress information periodically.

---

*CAM estimate: this is typically done by determining the estimate to complete (ETC) for each work package and summing it with the actual cost to date to produce the EAC.

22

Guidance information:

Sub-contractors should provide a periodic progress report which contains information relevant to the nature of the procurement (see Attribute 14 – supplier schedule integration). It is important that there is verification of the accuracy of the supplier information. This may be achieved during performance reviews with the supplier or by physical on site verification.

Attribute 21 – risk and opportunity management

Aim:

- To ensure that there is alignment between the risk management and earned value management processes.

Reason:

- The risk management processes within a project overlap with the EVM processes, particularly around unplanned work-scope and estimate at completion.

Guidance information:

Risk and opportunity management is an integral part of EVM and is concerned with managing threats to the baseline. The management of opportunity is concerned with improving performance against the baseline.

Earned value and risk and opportunity management are fully integrated into the project team's project management and control processes, and regular reviews which seek to maintain or improve this position are undertaken.

Approved and budgeted risk mitigation or opportunity realisation activities should be included in the baseline project master schedule. The consumption of management reserve should be tracked in relation to the remaining risk exposure of the project.

Attribute 22 – baseline change management

Aim:

- To ensure that changes to the performance measurement baseline (the 'baseline') are carried out in a timely and controlled manner.

Reason:

- The baseline should contain the complete, agreed scope of work. As projects progress change is inevitable; the introduction of these changes into the baseline must be controlled.

To ensure that the project is managed in a controlled manner it is important that all changes are embodied into the PMB in an orderly, controlled and documented manner. Change management addresses the controlled process whereby the project incorporates formal change, conducts internal replanning and adjusts past, present and future information to incorporate changes.

The baseline change process exists in order to ensure all requests for change are recorded, progressed and tracked in a timely manner. Change can be requested through four sources: the project, CAM, customer or sub-contractor. Where it impacts the baseline then the associated CAM must define the impacts on work-scope, schedule, budget and product configuration. The level of authority for approving PMB changes must be clearly defined in either the project management plan or a project control plan and any changes that are approved must be implemented within the PMB in a timely manner.

Budgets should not be transferred without corresponding work-scope. Change should also not be used to remedy or hide poor performance.

Attribute 23 – senior management usage

Aim:

- To ensure that EVM information is available to senior management to inform decision making during project, programme and portfolio reviews.

Reason:

- Senior management staff must have a basic understanding of EVM to be able to interpret the data that they receive. They may also need to be involved in providing project direction should variances become significant.

Guidance information:

Adopting the principle of management by exception, there may be times when senior management need to become involved in the project decision-making process. It is important that the senior management team have a clear understanding of EVM in project management and are able to interpret the information provided.

Attribute 24 – customer involvement

Aim:

- To ensure that EVM is operated in a manner that allows customer involvement.

Reason:

- To ensure that where the customer is involved, EVM is used in an open and transparent manner.

Guidance information:

The customer is typically the client or organisation that is funding the project.

The nature of customer involvement may be largely shaped by whether the customer has stated the requirement for EVM within the contract or if the project is using EVM as part of its standard company policy. If the customer has specified EVM, the expectation is that they have an active interest in EVM and would receive the relevant EVM reports. They would typically be involved in the decision-making process and be party to recovery planning.

EVM GOAL

Attribute 25 – EVM as a decision support tool

Aim:

- To ensure that EVM information forms a key component of project performance management reviews.

Reason:

- The value provided by EVM is achieved through using the data to make informed decisions. Producing EV data but not linking this to the decision-making process does not meet the aims of the process.

Guidance information:

The purpose of EVM is to provide management information to make better decisions. The EVM data should be used during project performance reviews to report the status of the project against the performance measurement baseline (PMB).

Variance to include explanation, impact, actions, summary from last period – so management can understand how this is affecting the project/ programme and show what has previously been done (from summary) – giving continuity of the issue and showing closure.

The requirement for a variance report is typically triggered by establishing cost, schedule and EAC thresholds. Variance reporting facilitates management by exception.

EVM compass questions

EVM foundations

	1	2	3	4	5	Comments	As is	To be
1. Earned value management competencies								
	Little or no training in the concepts of EVM is available and take-up is inconsistent.	Formal training and a budget to support its roll-out exists in the concepts of EVM for all key roles within the project organisation but take-up is inconsistent. There is little or no previous experience of EVM system implementation within the team.	Coordinated, funded training provides consistency in EVM approach and all team members have been sufficiently trained in EVM to fulfil their roles. Refresher and more advanced EVM training is provided to those that require it. The team is also able to draw upon the previous implementation experience of either team members or support personnel.	Training is linked into personnel development processes. Training and competency records are maintained. Previous experience of EVM system implementation is considered a crucial element when constructing project teams. Project teams are supported by staff with the knowledge to implement an appropriately scaled EVMS for the project and then support its use through initial months or data churn and review.	Training courses are tailored to meet specific project needs and the course materia is periodically updated to reflect lessons learnec from projects. These lessons are then directly fed into new projects when forming the teams.			
2. Sponsorship								
	The EVM system is established without the support or commitment of a senior manager.	The EVM system is established with the passive support of a senior manager.	The EVM sponsor provides proactive with visible support providing clear tactical direction.	The EVM sponsor provides strategic direction on the use of EVM across the business and into the customer and supplier chains.	EVM sponsorship and adoption is actively supported by all appropriate senior management team members.			

	1	2	3	4	5	Comments *As is* *To be*
3. Project level authorisation						
	The project has commenced with no formal authorisation documentation from the approval authority.	The approval authority have sanctioned the project using a formal process. Responsibility, accountability, and authority for delivering the project work scope are held by an authorised individual.	The project organisational structure is defined and documented, including the major subcontractors responsible for accomplishing the authorised work. Responsibility, accountability, and authority for project work scope are held by the senior project manager and delegated appropriately. Organisational responsibility is defined for all elements of working using an OBS. All activities are assigned to an element of the OBS. A documented correlation exists between the WBS and OBS, utilising the Responsibility Assignment Matrix (RAM).	Responsible managers (RMs) have fully documented scope, deliverables, budget, assumptions, and exclusions for their elements of work. The OBS is subject to formal change control. OBS and RAM are maintained.	This level considered and left blank.	
4. Work definition						
	There is no formal WBS or only an outline WBS exists.	Scope is documented and decomposed into meaningful, manageable elements. A recognised work breakdown structure and/or other appropriate structure e.g. product breakdown structure (PBS) is established.	All authorised work elements are defined for the project. A work breakdown structure (WBS) is used in this process. WBS elements are appropriately documented. The project objectives are clearly defined and documented and related to the WBS. The scope of work is under configuration control. The scope is documented in an auditable and traceable way (e.g. WBS dictionary).	A systematic process, such as using standard WBS structures to enable standardised reporting, decomposes project requirements and identifies the scope of work necessary to deliver these requirements. The link between customer requirements and WBS elements is clearly defined. The impact of changes to scope, technical specification or requirement are assessed for their impact on the WBS structure and its documentation.	The structure of the WBS is reviewed to ensure that future projects benefit from any lessons learned, particularly relating to how far it facilitated good dissemination of work products, collection of performance data and resulting ability to control the project.	

Organisation

27

(Continued on following page)

EVM basics

1	2	3	4	5	Comments	As is	To be
5. Detail work authorisation and budget assignment							
There is no mechanism for formal authorisation of work and budgets.	There is a formal mechanism for work authorisation but it is inconsistently applied and budget is not always associated with work scope.	The budget/work/schedule is formally authorised prior to work commencing. Task owners have formally agreed to complete the work as defined. Budgets are established (by control account or other authorised low-level account) for authorised work. Budgets are consistent with resources applied to schedules. Budget is distributed for duration of control accounts. Formal management procedures exist to open/close/suspend work but there is inconsistent application.	CAMs manage a total budget (£, $) and are responsible for material purchases as well as man-hours. Formal closure processes and mechanisms once the work scope has been completed and are consistently applied.	Budgets and actual cost are used to inform future estimating.			
6. Responsibility and accountability							
There are no personal terms of reference (TORs) issued that are appropriate to the project.	The senior project management team have been issued with appropriate TORs that have been communicated to all management staff within the organisation.	The project management team (inclusive of CAMs) have been issued with appropriate TORs that have been communicated to all management staff within the organisation. There are clear reporting lines to both the project management team and functional management where appropriate.	There is a change process/feedback in TORs and for the hand over of scope and budget between CAMs, which are maintained over the project life to provide consistency.	The individuals TORs are integrated with their respective HR personal development plans for personal objectives.			

					Comments
7. Material management					
Materials are excluded from the earned value management system (EVMS).	Material/consumables budgets are included in the EVMS and are separated into appropriate work and planning packages.	Material/consumables budgets are included in the EVMS with appropriate measures of progress and appropriate actual cost collection mechanisms are employed.	Materials/consumables can be traced from the purchase order requirement date through to the need date. Material costs within the EVMS can be traced to the purchase order.	Material/consumables budgets and actual cost are used to inform future estimating. Residual inventory has appropriate disposal controls within the EVMS.	
8. Basis of estimate					
There is an absence of estimating.	There is a record of the cost and schedule estimates but formal estimating techniques and processes have not been applied.	A formal structured estimate has been generated following standard estimating procedures. All cost and schedule estimating assumptions are fully documented.	Estimate is based on previous project norms, historical data, or parametric estimating. All estimating assumptions are fully documented.	The estimate has been reviewed by an independent authority. Upon completion of projects the actual performance data is used to inform future estimates/update project norms.	
9. Management reserve (cost and schedule)					
The authorised project budget does not contain any management reserve (MR).	The authorised project budget does contain an element for MR but can not be substantiated.	MR has been identified and can be substantiated by relation to the risk register and by using one or more of the following: - risk assessment/analysis - previous project outturns - industry norms - confidence modelling The change control process is used to manage changes to the MR.	The MR budget is managed on a regular basis in light of outstanding risks and opportunities. Confidence modelling is used on a regular basis to support the MR budget.	Metrics on the drawdown and use of MR are managed and fed back into the estimating and risk assessment standards.	
10. Supplier budget integration					
No supplier/partner budget data is entered into the project EVMS.	Supplier/partner budget data is entered into the project EVMS at a level inappropriate to the nature of the procured item.	Supplier/partner budget detail is entered into the project EVMS at a level appropriate to the nature of the procured item. The supplier/partner budget data within the project EVMS is appropriately aligned with the detailed information within the supplier/partner project management system (which could be an EVMS).	There is effective change control between the project and supplier/partner budgets ensuring that the baseline budget is aligned at all times.	There is full integration of commercial and project processes enabling a collaborative operating environment between the project and suppliers that is open to independent verification of performance.	

Organisation (rows 7–8) · *Budget* (rows 9–10)

(Continued on following page)

Schedule management

	1	2	3	4	5	Comments	As is	To be
				EVM basics				
11. Schedule structure and content								
	A time phased basis schedule exists but it contains little detail. Low-level and high-level activities are mixed. There are few logic linked activities. Constraints are used to achieve time phasing. If a variety of schedules exist it is not clear which has precedence.	There is a single time phased schedule but there is inconsistency in the use of logic, constraints and activity definition such that the validity of the critical path can not be substituted.	A time phased schedule exists at an appropriate level of detail structured or can be mapped to the WBS. The CP can be substantiated. Vertical and horizontal traceability can be demonstrated. The structure of the schedule supports an appropriate hierarchy of schedules. Artificial constraints are not used to replace logic. Supplier schedules are appropriately represented in the project schedule.	Supplier and customer schedules are vertically aligned. Creation of the project schedule is fully integrated with the project processes (e.g. baseline change, forecasting, risk, resource management) and the structure supports the management of the organisations portfolio of projects (including enterprise-wide resource planning, forecasting and risk mitigation activities).	Advanced scheduling techniques e.g. resource levelling, Monte Carlo schedule risk analysis are used systematically in optimising the schedule.			
12. Schedule resource allocation								
	The schedule is not resourced.	The schedule is partially resourced but not at the level that permits resource levelling to be effected.	Resources are defined to sufficient granularity allowing effective resource levelling to be conducted at activity level and this levelling has been performed.	The current version of the schedule is maintained to reflect future resource requirements throughout the life of the project and levelling is applied to demonstrate appropriate allocation.	The effectiveness of resource allocation is reviewed to ensure future resource optimisation and this is fully integrated with enterprise-wide resource planning.			

	1	2	3	4	5	Comments	As is	To be
13. Objectivity of EV progress assessment								
Schedule management	Formal earned value techniques (EVTs) are not used. Level of effort (LoE) accounts for the majority of the performance measurement baseline (PMB).	EV is assessed based on schedule percent complete or schedule work remaining. LOE is clearly identified but is inappropriately applied on discrete measurable tasks.	EV is related to physical products, milestones, technical performance goals, and/or other indicators used to measure progress. Their use extends to suppliers as appropriate. LOE is clearly identified and it is time phased to properly reflect when work will be accomplished. LOE can be segregated for reporting purposes. The EVT used for each work package is formally documented.	The amount of LOE is optimised appropriately for the project. Where discrete measures can not be identified apportioned effort is applied in preference to LOE. Formal documentation (such as the system description) exists stating how EVTs are determined and used (e.g. explaining how % complete is implemented).	EVTs are reviewed in light of project experience and this is fed back into the definition of EV measurement types and supporting metrics.			
14. Supplier schedule integration								
	Supplier/partner schedule standards are ill defined and there is irregular provision of schedule information from suppliers/partners.	Scheduling requirements are appropriately flowed-down to suppliers/partners. Baseline schedules are provided but are not incorporated into the baseline project master schedule.	Supplier/partner milestones and lead-times are incorporated into the baseline project master schedule. All dependencies between teams have been identified and documented.	There is effective change control between the project and supplier/partner schedules ensuring that the baseline and forecast schedules are aligned at all times.	Forecast schedules are reviewed and challenged with reference to industry norms and/or revised resource requirements and availability.			
15. Process documentation and consistency of application								
Process	Little or no process documentation exist to support the application of EVM.	Documented EVM processes exist but there is inconsistent adherence. The EVM processes are not integrated with the wider business processes.	A formal documented EVM process exists (e.g. a system description). There is consistent adherence to the processes. The EVM processes are fully integrated with other business and project processes. The EVMS processes are under configuration control.	Generic EVM processes may be tailored with guidelines to meet specific local requirements in the form of local project instructions for different projects. Any local project instructions are under configuration control.	Continuous monitoring of process application is in place. Poor process performance is isolated, and corrective action plans are implemented. Process improvements are identified and documented, and introduced under configuration control. Implementation of process changes are rolled out to users in a timely manner.			

(Continued on following page)

Execute EVM

	1	2	3	4	5	Comments	As is	To be
16. Actual cost collection								
	The process for actual cost are collection is not defined. Costs collected at the project level.	Costs (£) are collected at Control Account (CA) level on a monthly basis. There is inconsistent cost allocation and accuracy. Sub-contract or material costs are not always reported within the same accounting period as the associated earned value is claimed, leading to cost variance.	Costs (£ and units) are collected in the EVMS at CA level as a minimum on a monthly basis. There is a formal process for checking and correcting errors that ensures consistent, accurate cost allocation. The accounting policy for different cost types (e.g. overhead, G&A, direct, materials) is clearly defined and consistently applied. Subcontract or material costs are reported within the same accounting period as the associated earned value is claimed. Where material actuals are not available, estimated actuals or accruals are used.	Costs (£ and units) are collected in the EVMS at work package (WP) level as a minimum on a weekly basis. The 'actual cost' reflects accruals & commitments plus other defined adjustments and can be fully reconciled with the accounting systems.	Process adherence on cost collection using metrics is applied and systemic issues (e.g. timing) are corrected in a timely fashion.			
17. Schedule progress and control								
	The schedule is progressed in an inconsistent and irregular manner. There is no reference to performance against the baseline.	The schedule is consistently progressed based on work accomplished on a regular basis - at least monthly. There is no reference to performance against the baseline.	Regular variance analysis is performed on current schedule vs. baseline critical path and float analysis is conducted. Short term recovery planning is used on a monthly basis. On a monthly basis long term schedule forecast to completion is conducted.	Project schedules are reviewed and progressed on a weekly basis to redirect short term recovery plans where appropriate. Formal recovery plans are utilised to effect recovery action.	On a regular basis there is independent verification of progress to date and validation of the schedule to completion. Lessons learnt during these reviews are fed back into the scheduling processes.			

Execution

	1	2	3	4	5	Comments	As is	To be
18. Data integrity								
	There is little or no understanding of data integrity within the project. all data is treated as accurate without checks.	There is an unacceptable level of errors in output data (across earned value, actual cost and planned value data) that has a detrimental impact on the integrity of the project data set.	There is an acceptable level of errors in output data that has a minimal impact on the integrity of the project data set. Discrepancies are identified, assessed and managed.	The project actively attempts to reduce residual data integrity problems by measuring the quality and timeliness of the EV data using metrics.	There is full data integrity and errors are rare.			
19. Estimate of complete								
	The project EAC if produced at all is determined on an inconsistent and irregular basis.	The project EAC (generated either by management or systematically) is determined on a consistent and regular basis but can not be substantiated using detailed project data.	The project EAC (for cost and schedule out-turn) is determined at an appropriate level on a monthly basis, which is substantiated through lower level performance, risk mitigation and resources required to complete the remaining planned work.	Comparative forecasts (e.g. statistical EACs and TCPI) are produced and used to review the reasonableness of the project forecast. Potential EAC changes (with consideration to actions to manage future risks and opportunities) are documented and reviewed during the formal EAC cycle. 3 point EACs are generated at project level that can be substantiated.	There is independent validation of the EAC on a regular basis. EACs calculated on a time phased ETC based on: - the current schedule forecast; - resource requirements and availability; - past performance.; and - latest risk mitigation and opportunity realisation position.			
20. Supplier management and reporting								
	Supplier/partner reports performance and forecast on an irregular basis and to an inconsistent standard. No supplier data is being represented in the project EVM data.	Supplier/partner reports performance and forecast on a timely basis to an inconsistent standard. Supplier data is represented in the project EVM data, but may not be based on Information delivered from the supplier.	Supplier/partner reports performance and forecast on a timely basis to an inconsistent standard. Supplier performance data is verified by the project and is deemed to be reliable and accurately presented.	Regular supplier/partner performance reviews are conducted using the supplier/partner EV data as the basis of the review, with supporting variance analysis and corrective action planning. Verification is conducted at appropriate points within the schedule.	Suppliers are included in regular EV meetings and support variance analysis and corrective action planning. Suppliers are reviewed as part of the assurance process (e.g. IBR, DR, SR, maturity assessments).			

(Continued on following page)

Execute EVM

1	2	3	4	5	Comments	As is	To be
21. Risk and opportunity management							
Risk and opportunity management process not considered in the EV system.	Risk/opportunity management and earned value management processes are loosely linked. The data from the two processes are compared and contrasted but not reflected in either the baseline or monthly forecasts.	Approved risk mitigation/opportunity realisation activities are budgeted and included within the project schedule. The change process is utilised to approve and schedule new risk mitigation/opportunity realisation activities.	Risk and opportunity management and EV processes are integrated. Information provided on uncertainty and risks helps to determine the confidence the project baseline and forecast (including assessing the appropriateness of the remaining management reserve).	Processes are periodically reviewed and maturity metrics are used to drive continuous improvement.			
22. Baseline change management							
Baselines are not maintained. No formal process for incorporating or recording changes to the baseline exists.	Baseline changes are controlled by a documented process. Baselines are maintained inconsistently and irregularly. The process of change approval and embodiment is not timely. Inappropriate changes are applied to the baseline eg. frequent replans occur with the result of wiping out previously recorded variances and/or budget being transferred without the corresponding transfer of work.	Baseline changes are controlled by a documented process. Direct and consequential impact assessments are conducted by the project team. Approval is based on type of change and value. Baselines are maintained consistently and regularly. Process of change approval and embodiment is timely. Appropriate changes are applied to the baseline. Budget is not transferred without the corresponding transfer of work.	Direct and consequential impact assessments of changes are conducted, coordinated with and understood by the affected teams, functions and suppliers prior to approval.	Baseline changes are assessed and aligned with other project baselines (e.g. configuration, requirements) prior to approval. The performance of the baseline change process is periodically reviewed to ensure it is performing adequately and meeting the needs of all projects.			

1	2	3	4	5	Comments	As is	To be
23. Senior management usage							
There is negligible senior management understanding or review of the EV data.	The EVM performance data is reviewed on an irregular basis with only a limited understanding of the data by the senior management team.	The EVM performance data is reviewed on a regular basis with a good understanding/interpretation of the data by the senior management team, who commit to meaningful actions based on the data on an irregular basis.	The senior management team recognises the importance of the data, consistently understands what it is telling them, and commit to meaningful actions based on the data on a regular basis.	The senior management team uses the data as a key input to business decision making.			
24. Customer involvement							
The customer has little or no interest in EVM.	The customer provides passive support and requests monthly performance reports summarised to project level. The customer does not have the relevant EVM expertise but may have participated in EVM system reviews e.g. integrated baseline review.	The customer is involved in project EVM reviews and helps define and improve EVM reporting formats. The customer receives formal reports on a periodic basis from the EVM system. The information provided is at an agreed level of the WBS on performance trends, and corrective action plans. The customer has the relevant EVM expertise.	Customer representatives engage with project team opposite numbers in the ongoing review of project health, utilising EVM information. The customer is involved in EVM system reviews (e.g. IBRs, demonstration reviews and ongoing surveillance).	The customer is instrumental in supporting the development and usage of the EVM system. There is full transparency in project health (e.g. costs, variance analysis, progress, risks) and customer commitments.			
		EVM goal					
25. EVM as a decision support tool							
EV data is only used in the formal project review process on an irregular basis and/or is limited to only parts of the project work scope (e.g. critical path performance).	EV data is used on a consistent and regular basis to support formal project reviews. Management explain cause and impact of deviations from the baseline based on cost and schedule variance but formal variance reporting is not performed.	EV data forms a key element of the project review. Responsible managers explain cause and impact of deviations from the baseline using a formal variance analysis reporting (VAR) triggered by exceeding management set thresholds. The VAR is used to inform recovery planning.	Responsible managers review trends, performance indices and VARs to regularly inform recovery planning and to determine required future performance levels and associated resource requirements.	Efficacy, efficiency, and effectiveness of correction actions and management decisions are measured as part of the management feedback loop. Responsible managers address systemic problem areas.			

Conclusion

The EVM compass aims to provide organisations with a customisable framework that provides the base for ongoing assessments of projects, enabling continuous improvement of EVM practice and delivering real business benefit.

Annex A

Terminology and glossary

The definitions provided below are aligned to *Earned Value Management: APM Guidelines.*

Activity An element of work performed during the course of a project. An activity normally has an expected duration, an expected cost, and expected resource requirements. Activities are often subdivided into tasks.

Actual cost of work performed (ACWP) The costs actually incurred and recorded in achieving the work performed.

Actual cost The costs actually incurred and recorded in accomplishing work performed.

Actual time expended The elapsed time from the beginning of the task to date.

Allocated budget See *Total allocated budget*

Applied direct costs The actual direct costs recognised in the time period associated with the consumption of labour, material, and other direct resources, without regard to the date of commitment or the date of payment. These amounts are to be charged to work-in-process when any of the following takes place:

a. labour, material, or other direct resources are actually consumed;

b. material resources are withdrawn from inventory for use;

c. material resources are received that are uniquely identified to the contract; or

d. major components or assemblies that are specifically and uniquely identified to a single serially numbered end item are received on a line flow basis.

Apportioned effort Effort that, by itself, is not readily measured or divisible into discrete work packages but which is related in direct proportion to the planning and performance on other measured effort.

Authorised work All work performed, pursuant to the contract, within the contract price.

Authorised unpriced work (AUW) Includes work that has been authorised, but for which the cost has not been finalised by virtue of a formal contract amendment.

Baseline See *Performance measurement baseline.*

Budget The resources (in money and/or hours) assigned for the accomplishment of a specific task or group of tasks.

Budget at completion The total authorised budget for achieving the project scope of work. It is equal to the sum of all allocated budgets plus any undistributed budget (management reserve is not included.)

Budgeted cost for work performed (BCWP) The sum of the budgets for completed work packages and completed portions of open work packages, plus the applicable portion of the budgets for level of effort and apportioned effort.

Budgeted cost for work scheduled (BCWS) The sum of the budgets for all work packages, planning packages, etc. scheduled to be achieved (including in-process work packages), plus the amount of level of effort and apportioned effort scheduled to be achieved. This may be expressed as the BCSW within a given time period, such as period BCWS or cumulative BCWS.

Budgets for work packages. See *Work package budgets*.

Commitment That portion of purchased items or services which has been ordered, but for which no actuals have been incurred.

Contract budget base The contract target cost plus the estimated cost of authorised unpriced work.

Contract price The price payable by the customer under the contract for the proper delivery of the supplies and services specified in the scope of work of the contract.

Contract target cost The total of the sum of all control accounts plus undistributed budget plus management reserve.

Control account A management control point at which actual costs can be accumulated and compared to earned value and budgets (resource plans) for management control purposes. A control account is a natural management point for cost/schedule planning and control since it represents the work assigned to one responsible organisational element on one contract work breakdown structure (CWBS) element.

Control account manager The performing manager who is responsible for planning, performing, and monitoring the elements of work defined within that control account.

Cost performance report A contractually required report, prepared by the contractor, containing information derived from the internal system. Provides status of progress on the contract.

Cost variance A metric for the cost performance on a project. It is the algebraic difference between earned value and actual cost (CV = BCWP – ACWP.) A positive value indicates a favourable position and a negative value indicates an unfavourable condition.

Critical path method A network analysis technique used to predict project duration by analysing which sequence of activities (which path) has the least amount of scheduling flexibility (the least amount of float). Early dates are calculated by means of a forward pass using a specified start date. Late dates are calculated by means of a backward pass starting from a specified completion date (usually the forward pass's calculated project early finish date).

Direct costs The costs of resources expended in the achievement of work, which are directly charged to the project, without inclusion of indirect costs.

Distributed budget All budgets that have been assigned to the control accounts. Distributed budget excludes management reserve and undistributed budget.

Earned value The value of completed work expressed in terms of the budget assigned to that work.

Earned value management (EVM) A best practice project control process that is based on a structured approach to planning, cost collection and performance measurement. It facilitates the integration of project scope, schedule, cost, risk and resource objectives and the establishment of a baseline plan for performance measurement.

Earned value management system (EVMS) An integrated management system which uses earned value to measure progress objectively.

Earned value techniques (EVT) The technique used to objectively assess progress.

Estimate at completion (EAC) Actual direct costs, plus indirect costs allocatable to the contract, plus the estimate of costs (direct and indirect) for remaining authorised work.

Estimate to completion (ETC) The forecast of labour hours and costs required to complete the remaining authorised work. It is based on a bottom-up analysis of remaining work in which consideration of past and future performance, along with the availability of resources, is taken into consideration.

Forecast cost at completion See *Estimate at completion*.

Funding Funding represents the actual money available for expenditure in the achievement of contract work. The planning of work and the time-phasing of budgets and estimates to completion (ETCs) should be consistent with the known available funding for that period.

Indirect costs The costs for common or joint objectives which cannot be identified specifically with a particular project or activity. Also referred to as overhead cost or burden.

Initial budget See *Original budget*.

Integrated baseline review (IBR) An IBR is a formal process conducted to assess the content and integrity of the performance measurement baseline (PMB). The purpose of the IBR is to achieve and maintain a project and customer understanding of the risks inherent in the PMB and the management control processes that will operate during its execution.

Latest revised estimate See *Estimate at completion*.

Level of effort (LOE) Effort of a general or supportive nature which does not produce definite end products. Earned value (budgeted cost for work performed) for LOE always equals the planned budget to date (budgeted cost for work scheduled) whether or not any work is performed.

Management reserve (MR) An amount of the total allocated budget withheld for management control purposes rather than designated for the achievement of a specific task or set of tasks. It is not a part of the performance measurement baseline.

Material The term to encompass all non-labour classes of resource.

Milestone An activity of zero duration principally used to enhance the clarity of the programme structure.

Network diagram Any schematic display of the logical relationships of project activities. Always drawn from left to right to reflect project chronology.

Organisational breakdown structure. A functionally oriented code established to identity the performance responsibility for work on a specific contract.

Original budget The budget established at, or near, the time the contract was signed, based on the negotiated contract cost.

Original duration The duration established at, or near, the time the contract was signed, based on the negotiated contract cost.

Other direct costs (ODC) A group of costs which can be identified to specific tasks, other than labour, material and subcontract. Included in ODC are such costs as travel, accommodation, insurance, computer time and services.

Overhead Indirect labour, material, supplies, services costs and other charges, which cannot be consistently identified with individual projects. See *Indirect costs*.

Over target baseline When remaining budgets are deemed insufficient to complete the remaining work, the budgets may be increased by seeking approval in advance from the customer. Work is then be done to a new total budget which exceeds the original contract budget base, or an over target baseline. Now the total allocated budget equals the previous contract budget base (CBB) plus the previously budgeted margin plus any contractor contribution.

Performance measurement baseline (PMB) The time-phased budget plan against which contract performance is measured. It is formed by the budgets assigned to scheduled control accounts and the applicable indirect budgets. For future effort, not planned to the control account level, the performance measurement baseline also includes budgets assigned to higher level CWBS elements and undistributed budgets. It equals the total allocated budget less management reserve.

Performing organisation A defined unit within the contractor's organisation structure, which applies the resources to perform the work.

Period A defined block of time that forms the financial and reporting calendar for an EVM system. Typically weekly or monthly.

Planning package A logical aggregation of work within a control account, normally the far-term effort, that can be identified and budgeted in early baseline planning, but is not yet defined into work packages.

Product breakdown structure (PBS) A hierarchical structure, which breaks down the product into its constituent parts, in a similar way to a bill of materials.

Responsible organisation A defined unit within the contractor's organisational structure which is assigned responsibility for achieving specific tasks.

Responsibility assignment matrix A depiction of the relationship between the contract work breakdown structure elements and the organisations assigned responsibility for ensuring their accomplishment.

Rolling wave The action of converting a planning package into a work package.

Schedule The timing and sequence of tasks within a project, as well as the project duration. The schedule consists mainly, of tasks, dependencies among tasks, durations, constraints, resources and time-oriented project information.

Schedule variance A metric for the schedule performance on a program. It is the difference between earned value and the budget (schedule variance = earned value - budget). A positive value is a favourable condition while a negative value is unfavourable.

Significant variances Those differences between planned and actual performance, which require further review, analysis, or action. Appropriate thresholds should be established as to the magnitude of variances that will automatically require variance analysis.

Statement of work A narrative description of products or services to be delivered by the project.

Supplies The goods and services including intellectual property required to be supplied under the contract.

Total allocated budget The sum of all budgets allocated to the contract. Total allocated budget consists of the performance measurement baseline plus all management reserve. The total allocated budget reconciles directly to the contract budget base.

Undistributed budget Budget applicable to contract effort that has not yet been allocated into the performance measurement baseline or placed in reserve.

Variance at completion The difference between the total budget assigned to a contract, WBS element, organisational entity or control account, and the estimate at completion. It represents the amount of expected overrun or underrun.

Variances See *Significant variances*.

Work breakdown structure (WBS) A product-oriented family tree division of hardware, software, services and other work tasks which organises, defines, and graphically displays the product to be produced as well as the work to be done to achieve a specified product.

a. **Project summary work breakdown structure** A summary WBS tailored to a specific defence material item by selecting applicable elements from one or more summary WBSs or by adding equivalent elements unique to the project.

b. **Contract work breakdown structure (CWBS)** The complete WBS for a contract, developed and used by a contractor within the guidelines of MIL-STD-881 and according to the contract work statement. The CWBS includes the levels specified in the contract.

Work breakdown structure (WBS) dictionary A description of all individual elements within each level of the WBS which is sufficient to define their scope, including tasks, dependencies and deliverables.

Work-package budgets Resources, which are formally assigned by the contractor to achieve a work package, expressed in dollars, hours, standards or other measurable units.

Work-packages Detailed short-span jobs, or material items identified by the contractor for achieving work required to complete the contract.

Annex B

Related documents

In using the APM EVM compass the following documents provide additional information.

1. Association for Project Management (2008) *Earned Value Management: APM Guidelines* ISBN: 978-1-903494-26-4
2. Association for Project Management (2008) *Interfacing Risk and Earned Value Management* ISBN: 978-1-903494-24-0
3. Association for Project Management (2006) *APM Body of Knowledge, 5th edition* ISBN: 978-1-903494-13-4